About the Author

After scraping his way through college, Larry landed a job at a big oil company. He was still a naïve, idealistic nerd and didn't really know what he had gotten himself into. Big Oil expected him to conform to their plan for his career, as countless engineers before him had. Pursuing his own path got him into a lot of trouble and lead to several job and location changes. He recognized early on how his industry was contributing to the pollution of our environment, but could do nothing about it. All this finally changed after he got a job where oil companies were his clients, not his employers. And later, he became involved in a biofuel technology that really could help make the world a cleaner place.

Larry Dean lives with his wife and two cats in Wild and Wonderful Charleston, West Virginia.

An Einganeer's Tale

Larry Dean

An Einganeer's Tale

Olympia Publishers
London

www.olympiapublishers.com
OLYMPIA PAPERBACK EDITION

Copyright © Larry Dean 2024

The right of Larry Dean to be identified as author of
this work has been asserted in accordance with sections 77 and 78 of
the Copyright, Designs and Patents Act 1988.

All Rights Reserved

No reproduction, copy or transmission of this publication
may be made without written permission.
No paragraph of this publication may be reproduced,
copied or transmitted save with the written permission of the publisher,
or in accordance with the provisions
of the Copyright Act 1956 (as amended).

Any person who commits any unauthorised act in relation to
this publication may be liable to criminal
prosecution and civil claims for damage.

A CIP catalogue record for this title is
available from the British Library.

ISBN: 978-1-80439-840-1

This book is a memoir. It reflects the author's present recollections of
experiences over time. Some names and characteristics have been
changed, some events have been compressed, and some dialogue
has been recreated.

First Published in 2024

Olympia Publishers
Tallis House
2 Tallis Street
London
EC4Y 0AB

Printed in Great Britain

For Pampers

Acknowledgements

Bill Tromans, St. Albans, England—a friend and colleague who has always been my go-to guy for proofreading the many manuals and technical papers I've written. Although you failed to teach me any proper King's English, I am grateful for the many corrections you suggested.

Rick Von Flatern, Austin, Texas—a friend and professional technical editor. Thank you for still allowing my VOICE in your editing of my manuscript. I still owe you those two beers.

Cary Trierweiler, Wesley Chapel, Florida—my niece. Thank you for the corrections and suggestions you made after reading my final proof. You say you are not a grammar X-SPURT, but you are!

Well do you know he put Algernon in a box like a big tabel with alot of twists and terns like all kinds of walls and a START and a FINISH like the paper had. Only their was a skreen over the big tabel. And Bert took out his clock and lifted up a slidding door and said lets go Algernon and the mouse sniffd 2 or 3 times and startid to run. First he ran down one long row and then when he saw he coudnt go no more he came back where he startid from and he just stood there a minit wiggeling his wiskers. Then he went off in the other direction and startid to run again.

It was just like he was doing the same thing Bert wanted me to do with the lines on the paper. I was laffing because I thot it was going to be a hard thing for a mouse to do. But Algernon kept going all the way threw that thing all the rite ways till he came out where it said FINISH and he made a squeek. Bert says that means he was happy because he did the thing rite.

-- Daniel Keyes, from *Flowers for Algernon*

Contents

Chapter 1 Gear 13

Chapter 2 My Last Summer 18

Chapter 3 Diving In 26

Chapter 4 Hooked 40

Chapter 5 Upstream 49

Chapter 6 Back Downstream 58

Chapter 7 My Sweet Spot 64

Chapter 8 Home 73

Chapter 1
Gear

"My daddy's an einganeer!" My son's response whenever asked, "What's your father do?" He had no idea what an einganeer was (but I believe he thought it might have something to do with trains).

I'm not sure he or my other two know to this day what their einganeer daddy did. (Telling them is one reason I have for writing this book). But they sure knew that they didn't want to be one. They all got as far away from it as they could, all going instead into: THE ARTS: one into music, one into theater, and one into… the Navy.

Me being an einganeer was really tough on my family. Seems like we moved every three years or so. Thank God all our moves were only in the US. Although they tried to make me do so once, I drew the line at moving overseas (more about this later). But if you're gonna move up in the company, you gotta move on, to wherever the hell they tell ya—and I was one ambitious son of a bitch.

Still, the family stuck with me—they're all screwed up, but they stuck with me. It's now just me and my wife of almost fifty years, living a life of retired bliss and letting all the memories of my attempts to solve the problems of this world melt away like glacier ice. Which brings up another reason for my writing this book: getting all this stuff down on paper before I forget it. Never mind that my memory has already become 'selective'.

In addition to my family, I wrote this book for all those Howard Wolowitz's of the world—those under-appreciated engineers who yearn for the recognition they so richly deserve but never quite seem to get it. Those Scotty's who always get overruled by the bosses who want to 'explore new worlds', no matter how many warnings of catastrophe they give them.

There are no Emmys for engineers. No televised events with red carpets and evening gowns. Sure, lots of companies and engineering groups give out nice engraved acrylic obelisks and pyramids, some even with encasements of various organic materials. But Who Cares? I've got a few up in a closet somewhere. They aren't worth anything. And if you try to tell someone what they were given to you for, they politely smile and walk away.

The writers of *The Big Bang Theory* used Howard to show their viewers what being an under-appreciated engineer is all about. Yes, they gave him some fame by making him an astronaut—but only after first mocking him as the inventor of the anti-gravity toilet. Any engineer would *and should* be very proud of such an important invention, an invention that truly contributed to the possibility of extended manned space flight.

But what did Howard get? Ridiculed. The more Howard talked to his friends about his achievements, the more they wanted him to just go away. One episode magnificently showed that even real astronauts have the same problem (Buzz Aldrin, handing out moon pies on Halloween to Trick-or-Treaters who couldn't care less who he was!).

Many times, throughout my career, I was told that I need to 'toot my own horn' more. I've always found that hard to do. Nobody really wants to hear me spout off about something they know and care little about. "Okay, so you had something to do with something that was a problem; that ain't a problem no more. So what's the big deal?" If you have to go into trying to explain your accomplishment, you've lost. They politely smile and walk away—or take your moon pie and run. It's so much easier to keep quiet and just go on with life.

* * *

Engineers are first and foremost PROBLEM SOLVERS. But after a problem is solved, it's gone. Ever try telling a Gen Z'er about the days before cell phones? If they do happen to listen, the most you can expect to get from them is sympathy for your having to live through such a dark time.

I guess there's really nothing wrong with a solved problem disappearing from mankind's consciousness—but the SOMEONE who solved the problem also gets forgotten. I'm reminded of that big guy in the Tom Hanks movie 'The Green Mile'. He would visibly struggle to absorb someone else's problem and thereby make things better for people, but get nothing in return. In fact, they even executed him at the end. Yeah, I can relate.

Being a problem solver is also a curse. Many people (like my wife) don't want you to actually solve their problem—but only listen to them tell you about it. That's hard for an engineer like me to do. I hear a problem and I immediately go into Problem Solving Mode. I begin spewing out solutions that are neither appreciated, nor supportive, nor sympathetic. Then I sleep on the couch.

And then there's the unavoidable tendency for an engineer like me to offer solutions to problems greater than himself. He believes he has all the answers to every question about politics, religion, immigration, policing, the environment—you name it! He could solve all these problems and make the world a better place if only someone would listen to him. But all he gets for his superior intellect is ulcers, high blood pressure, and folks calling him a weirdo.

A few engineers still do gain fame and get books written about them—the famous nerds who have built or invented something big or important enough that normal people would know about it and appreciate it—guys like Edison, Einstein, Gates, and Jobs. They won't get anything out of reading this book.

I once knew a guy who worked with Jobs during those early days. He claimed he was the real brains behind his ideas, and gave me reasons to believe him. His creativity and ability to think 'outside the box' was truly phenomenal. He died in a log cabin on a river in West Virginia. I've written this book for him and guys like him.

I realize that engineers are not the only workers who suffer the pains of under-appreciation. I know there are also nurses, waiters, plumbers, roofers, teachers, clerks, cashiers, etc. etc. who go home each night feeling used. Who feel they aren't making a difference in this world, no matter how hard they work. Although the subject and setting is different, as well as the journey, the story's the same. This book is also for them.

* * *

As the title states, this is a TALE. According to Vocabulary.com, a tale is: *"A story, especially one that's full of creative embellishments. Tales can be true or fictional, but they generally consist of a narrative with a beginning and an end, made more interesting and exciting with vivid details."* Oh, there will be creative embellishments and vivid details… and most everything in this book is true, sort of.

The story is about my career—a five-decade journey with ups and downs, comedy (lots of comedy) and drama, laughs and tears. I also hope it leaves you with some thoughts about our environment and my contribution to screwing it up or helping to save it, depending on your perspective.

You have begun reading a masterpiece (the first creative embellishment in this book). Although it's about an engineer, I promise it won't get too technical. If you come across anything you don't understand, stop reading and send me a nasty note.

Oh, I almost forgot my disclaimer: *I've withheld the names of people and companies in my little tale to avoid pissing them off. If anyone thinks they know who or where I'm talking about, you're wrong.*

So, as Mom always told me (and now that I think about it, it makes no sense): "Get your TALE in gear boy!"

Chapter 2
My Last Summer

"But, Mom, this is my last summer"—not a particularly good excuse for getting out of stuff I didn't want to do. It just brought on an "Aww, poor baby, now get your butt off the couch!"

I've been kidded about the 'My Last Summer' claim all my life. But that summer, after high school and before college, was indeed my last summer. Every year before then, I so looked forward to those three months of no-school freedom. Every year since then, I've spent those three months going to school or fulfilling other adult obligations.

I wish I could say that I was always interested in learning how things worked while growing up and that my superior understanding of math and sciences naturally led me to study engineering—but, truth be told, I became an engineer to avoid Vietnam. Not proud of it, but them's the facts. Going to Canada would have been my second choice, but I wasn't ready to be that much on my own.

I had occasionally joined my father when he worked at Fort Lewis, the last US base most soldiers bound for Nam saw. I still remember the faces I saw there. I wanted no part of it.

I remember Walter Cronkite reporting the Viet Cong body count each night, and how it was a good thing that it was thousands more than ours. I remember Walter telling me about Mai Lai, and how my fifteen-year-old mind struggled to comprehend that such a thing was even possible.

I remember a family friend who came back from Nam with PTSD before PTSD was a thing. He had been like an older brother to me. Now he was distant and sad. No way I was going to follow him.

So, I managed to get something called a 2S deferment, somehow convincing folks that I would be more valuable to society as a student than killing Commies. Good thing too. Shortly thereafter, I saw live on TV that my favorite day of the year, my birthday, now meant I would have been in the fifth group of eighteen-year-olds next inducted that year.

They still did send me a notice to report, but since I was already enrolled in college with the deferment, I was able to fight it. (Thank you, Mom, for starting me in kindergarten when I was four.) But there was one catch. To keep the deferment, I had to maintain at least a 3.0 GPA. Somehow, I managed to make it through with a three point two. *Whoopee doo.*

* * *

I was never a very good student. When I first learned to write, I wrote backwards. And this was way before Stephen King used REDRUM in *The Shining* to show that my talent was really an indication of superior intuition. I was just weird.

I was fortunate, though, to have a second-grade teacher (Miss FOCKNER—I hated her) who never gave up on me. (*Whoops! I broke my own disclaimer. That is her real name. What a witch!*) She turned me around, literally.

But I think all this did point to a flaw in my DNA that would forever make learning a little more difficult for me. Nothing anyone could put their finger on, but I felt I had to study twice as hard as everyone else to keep up with them.

Folks talk about their wonderful college days and how kids should go to college if for no other reason than for the wonderful experience. Now, looking back on it, those four years (and three summers) was the worst most stressful time of my life.

The exams that all seemed to require all-nighters. The always being evaluated by instructors, as well as upper-classmen and peers. The always being broke, even though I was working whenever I was not studying, pedaling candy in machines all over campus (pun intended; a bicycle was involved). I lived on Jell-O and macaroni—foods which turn water into something you could chew.

College life was not friendly to this geek. I was definitely not fraternity material, but then was shunned by most everyone at my assigned men's dorm. My only friend was a pet rat I had stolen from the psych lab. This did not help with my assimilation into dormitory living.

I named my pet *Algernon* after Daniel Keyes' book, *Flowers for Algernon*. It's about inferior beings seeking intelligence. Seemed a fitting description of my college aspirations.

Moving off-campus with a couple other geeks finally did help my living situation some. I soon, however, learned why folks don't like living with geeks.

After that last day in June, all I wanted was to get away from there as fast as I could before someone changed their mind. "Mail me the @#$%& diploma—no way I'm going back there to walk on a stage and have someone give it to me with a smile and a handshake! I'm through with schoolin'!"

So I thought. Actually, my schoolin' was only about to begin. College only tells others you know how to learn, not that you know anything. The real schoolin' starts in the real world. I now realize that I used very little of what I actually learned in college after I graduated.

* * *

I started college as a chemical engineering major. I liked high school chemistry, so thought maybe I had a special knack for it.

College chemistry kicked my butt—but I did pass, barely. Next up was ORGANIC Chemistry. No way would I pass that! And my 'advisor' made that abundantly clear to me. So I 'dropped' into mechanical. Little did I know at the time that most of my future career would revolve around organic chemistry.

My college offered three engineering fields of study, and there was definitely a pecking order to them. Chemical engineering was the top in terms of the one with the highest earnings potential. Mechanical was one step below. And if you still couldn't cut it, there was Civil.

Oh, there was also a fourth, on a plane all its own: Electrical. But it was so different from the others that no one was sure what they did was really engineering. They were the nerds to the rest of us nerds.

Something I found odd at college, there were no girl engineering students (well, except for a couple ugly ones in civil). Girls had always been the best in math and sciences through high school, so at first, I thought "Great, less competition!" I had forgotten that in high school, girls weren't competition, but often the reason I got through. They were always the best study partners and tutors.

I guess having no girls around did mean there was less of a 'distraction', if you know what I mean. But not in the way you probably think. Nerds don't go to college to meet women—well, except for the creepy ones. (You can take that last statement either way). I definitely wasn't there for romance. And since college girls don't go looking for guys among the engineering nerds, it was never a problem.

Like most nerds, I felt clumsy around girls. My first attempt at French kissing grossed her out. (I guess I shouldn't have led with that). Then backing into her parent's fence while speeding out of her driveway cemented the experience in my mind for life. Having no girls around at college was indeed helpful.

* * *

Mechanical engineering has two tracks of study: fluids and machines; stuff that moves, and things that makes stuff move. Problem is most people only think machines when asked what mechanical engineers do. No surprise since it is called MECHNICAL engineering. DUH!

The Machineers get into studying stress and strains, vibrations and torques, materials and loads, pulleys and gears. They become the doctors of machinery.

I fought my way through these courses, hoping I'd never have to actually practice the profession. I surely would get sued for malpractice.

Later on, in the real world, I learned that machine doctoring really isn't that difficult. There's something called the *Redneck's Repair Kit* that prescribes the only two medicines necessary: duct tape and WD40. If it moves and ain't supposed to, use duct tape. If it's supposed to move but doesn't, use WD40.

The Fluideers get into studying gases and liquids, pressures and temperatures, lift and drag, motion and flow, and energy. I really got into the energy thing. I liked saying words like THRUST.

The two Laws of Thermodynamics: 1) everything eventually becomes garbage, and 2) energy can be changed, but not made – seemed to me like rules to live by—so "Lord of the Rings" like.

Add to these Sir Isaac Newton's three Laws of Motion: 1) nothing moves unless pushed, 2) bigger things must be pushed harder, and 3) everything pushes back with the same force it was pushed with – and you've got all you need to define nature, as far as I was concerned.

The overwhelming majority of guys in my mechanical engineering class were machineers. These were the driveway tinkerers, the daddy helpers, and the soap box boy scouts. They knew what they wanted when they signed up.

Most of the remaining fluideers in my class were into things like flight, steam, and hydraulics. These were the pilot want-a-bees, the power junkies, and the physics student dropouts who wanted to make some money without having to get a doctorate and teach.

That left me, in a minority of a minority. I should have stayed in chemical.

Upon graduation, each of us had a choice to make: Big Oil, or Big Steel? California or Pennsylvania? At that time, there were companies in each industry willing to hire everyone in our class, sight unseen. I chose Big Oil. Given that Big Steel has disappeared, seems I made the right decision. And later, I managed to retire before Big Oil is due to follow Big Steel into industry oblivion.

I like to think that maybe I had just a little to do with Big Oil being able to hold on for so long. Who knows? Had I gone with Big Steel, maybe the rust belt would still be shining. Maybe more folks would know why Pittsburg's football team is called the Steelers. Maybe more coal miners would still have jobs.

So anyway, off I went. My life was starting anew. I graduated, got married, and moved to California all in one week, exactly four years after the first week of my last summer.

* * *

I guess I should say something about that 'got married' statement. It had nothing to do with me holding a sign saying 'Marry Me and go to California'—although back then, that probably would have worked too.

They say there's someone for everyone, even us einganeers. I don't know about that, but I did have a girlfriend through my college years. Problem was, she was still back home in high school. I met her during my last summer, while working at the grocery store that first introduced me to the corporate world. (That was also the only time in my life that I actually belonged to a labor union).

I guess I had her swayed by my debonair nature. To her, I was a BMOC (Big Man On Campus). Her college boy sweetheart that was just far enough away to not burden her with everyday activities, but close enough to eagerly anticipate the next time we'd be together.

I was still an awkward nerd, but with her, it didn't seem to matter. She thought my brown Chevy Vega was hot, especially after I decorated it with gold peel-n-stick pin striping. She was okay with going to see the nerdy '50s band Sha Na Na on our first date. She fell for my cheesy pickup line, "Wanna see my cat?" (I didn't introduce her to Algernon until our second date). As Forrest Gump, the greatest nerd ever to grace the Silver Screen, said: "We were like peas and carrots."

No one in the dorm believed she existed until she came to

visit on Parents' Weekend as my mother. (We never got caught). After that, she was forever called Pampers (something about her being so much younger than me). My dorm mates could find nothing else wrong with her to torment me with. She was perfect, and they were jealous.

Pampers and I now have great-grandbabies in Pampers. I occasionally still call her Pampers, but then she hits back by calling me Depends (something about her being so much younger than me).

Chapter 3
Diving In

"You have REACTORS?"—my reaction when the company recruiter casually mentioned the word during my welcoming lunch the day before my first day. I had taken one nuclear engineering elective at college. I didn't get much out of it, but I did learn what a reactor was. The thought of working where there were atomic bombs in concrete boxes with guys like Homer Simpson looking after them terrified me!

I came to learn later that a reactor is actually any vessel (big cylindrical things) in the refinery where a chemical reaction is going on. "Oh, okay. No big deal then." I felt kind of stupid. But then, later on, I learned that many of these vessels were operating at astronomical pressures and temperatures and were subject to 'hot spots' that could melt through the vessel wall and to something called 'hydrogen blistering' which could blow a hole through the wall. So they were really just as dangerous as a nuclear reactor! What kept them from blowing up? Those guys in the control room, many of whom did remind me of Homer.

My first assignment was in the Environmental Engineering department. The department had two members—me and my boss. I think my boss got the job because his first name was Forrest. He had no other qualification to be a department manager, which is why they put him there by himself. He was so happy to finally have someone he could boss around.

My thoughts were *Oh Boy! I get to help clean up the world!*

I soon learned, though, that my job was not to clean up the world, but to make it as dirty as I could get away with. And all the world was available to me: air, sea, and land.

Refineries have these things called flares. You might have seen these towering candles casting a glow over your neighborhood refinery. Its job is to incinerate whatever is sent to it, and everything in the refinery has a path to the flare.

If something needs to be cleaned out, send its contents to the flare. If a pressure gets too high somewhere, relieve it to the flare. If it ain't worth screwing with, send it to the flare.

When its flame is that nice blue color, it's doing a good job, turning all the bad stuff into 'harmless' carbon monoxide and carbon dioxide. But when it's bright orange, it ain't doing so good. Some bad stuff is getting past it, and there could be a ghastly smell and black soot. There were many times I had to dust off my car before driving home.

For some reason, the state felt they had to set up monitors around the refinery and fine us whenever we had more than X violations each month. One of my jobs was to keep us at X—no more… and no less.

I wasn't very good at my job. We soon started budgeting for fines. Paying the fines was cheaper than improving the flare system.

*　*　*

Our waste water was sent back into the bay after it had been properly treated, of course. I was told that it was cleaner going back than it was when we sucked it out of the bay, but I never believed that.

Water was used throughout the refinery, mostly to cool stuff down from those astronomical temperatures. Hot water was then either sent to a furnace to be turned into steam or sent to the Cooling Tower, an enormous structure in which the water was cascaded over thousands of boards while giant fans sucked up air.

Various chemicals got added to the water everywhere to help some things and prevent others. They were supposed to do things like keep things from growing and clogging stuff up, make separating oil and water easier, and keep things from corroding. To do the latter, they'd either create a protective film (slime) that would stick on everything or keep the 'water' from turning into acid. Of course none of these chemicals ever made it into the bay with our waste water. Yeah right.

The guys selling all these chemicals to us were really nice. They'd give me stuff, take me to lunch, and invite me to visit their suites at conventions. Each one of them claimed to have better snake oils than the others. We were switching from one chemical vendor to another every few months or so to keep their competition going strong (and the gifts coming). We never saw one being any better than the other, and they all cost about the same.

* * *

Any water that couldn't be recycled got sent to the API SEPERATOR—as well as any rainfall or wash water, since these might have picked up some oily gunk off the ground. Since the American Petroleum Institute would put its name on it, this big scummy pond must be a good thing.

The API Separator tried to separate oil out of the water by gravity. Because oil is lighter than water, it's supposed to separate out, like a fine vinaigrette salad dressing. Well, in an oil refinery, it doesn't. But adding chemicals called emulsion breakers did help a lot.

Emulsion breakers are said to be BIODEGRADABLE, so they aren't supposed to hurt the environment. Yeah right.

As you probably know, BIO means LIFE. So biodegradable means decomposed by a life form, such as bacteria. That may well be true for toilet paper, but for this stuff, I think a better word for it might be BIODEGRADING. It degrades life.

Emulsion breakers do get eaten by bacteria, which gets eaten by fungi, which becomes plankton, which gets eaten by everything from clams to whales. All fine and good, right? Problem is, emulsion breakers contain toxins that may well end up on your dinner plate. But they sure did help the API Separator do a better job.

The scum floating on top of the API Separator periodically got sucked off by Hoovers (big vacuum trucks). Hoovers were also used to suck up gunk that fell to the bottom of the pond.

The 'water' in the middle was then sent to the DAFfy or Dissolved Air Flotation Unit (I added the 'fy'). The DAFfy was a big Jacuzzi that created a frothy brown foam, which also got sucked off by hoovers.

So out of the DAFfy, you got 'clean' water. And the black gooey gunk now filling the Hoovers, we called SLUDGE.

The 'clean' water was sent back to the bay, but not until it had been thoroughly tested, of course. The test was to run some of it through a fish tank. If all the fish died, something was seriously wrong. If a few died, no big deal. Each morning, THE FISH COUNT was reported to everyone. It took me a while to learn that it had nothing to do with the morning catch.

We were allowed to have no more than X fish die each day.

One of my jobs was to keep us at X—no more, no less. I wasn't very good at my job. Many fish died.

* * *

And then there's the sludge. It would have been best to just run it back through with the crude oil. But that would have taken up capacity better filled with pure crude oil. Sludge would have made the crude oil cruddier than it already was.

So, what could be done with this black, gooey, toxic stuff? Shipping it off for proper disposal would have been way too expensive. So someone had a brilliant idea. "Since sludge is biodegradable, let's just spread it on the ground!" We would call the operation SLUDGE FARMING, and I was to be its farmer.

I was to drive loaded Hoovers off to the far reaches of the refinery property where there was nothing but wilderness for as far as you could see (Google now shows homes built there), and spray this stuff onto the ground so the bugs in the soil could feast on it. And so another toxin journey through the 'Circle of Life' can begin.

To make sure there were enough bugs and that they'd get excited about being drenched with sludge, I also sprinkled the area with industrial sized bags of RID-X. This is the same stuff you flush down your toilet if you have a septic tank. I guess eating sludge is the same as eating shit if you're a bug.

Anyway, I was praised for having solved a major problem in the refinery. But I really didn't feel too good about it. Thank God a 50-foot bug never evolved from eating that stuff!

* * *

The public did see enough things to know that they didn't like refineries. We occasionally got bomb scare calls. Security wasn't very good back then, so a bomb could have been planted anywhere. But since it was easy for anyone to just make a phone call, they all turned out to be false alarms. Well, there was one real one once that made a lot of noise but caused no damage. Good to know that firecrackers won't bust steel pipe.

But whenever we got one of these calls – nights, weekends, holidays—the new (dispensable?) engineers were sent out to search for it by 'walking the lines'—while humming Johnny Cash and praying. It's ironic to think that the pipes we were walking on contained more explosives than anyone could have planted anywhere.

Thank God the activists back then were too dumb to know that the best place to plant their firecrackers was not on the pipes themselves, but on top of the 'floating' roof tanks they went to. These roofs literally float on top of gasoline, and leak all sorts of volatile vapors around their edge. A spiral stairway is conveniently provided for ready access to each.

* * *

Near the end of my first year, all the Homers decided they weren't being paid enough, so they went on strike. Our brilliant management said, "That's okay, the engineers can run the refinery." So for the next thirty days, that's what we did. On day thirty-one, the Homers came back to work, and got everything they had asked for.

Because of the picket line, we were locked in, working twelve hour shifts seven days a week. We were, however, given the opportunity to go home once a week, for a 'conjugal' visit.

Having to be escorted through the picket line by guys with guns didn't deter anyone.

Just so happens that I had a newborn at home at the time, our first born. So to help my wife out in my absence, I flew out someone who I knew had extensive experience with infants and would assure that my wife made no mistakes—my mother. Not a good idea. Need I say more?

Since I was still pretty new, they didn't put me where I could do much damage (so they thought). I was assigned to the marine terminal. (Fancy name for a dock. There was nothing TERMINAL about it).

Gotta say, I had the time of my life. I got to channel my inner 'On the Waterfront' Marlon Brando into my job: *"I coulda had class. I coulda been a contender. I coulda been somebody, instead of a bum."*

I was a longshoreman, of sorts. I got to tie up ships and barges to the dock, line up pipes and pumps so stuff would come from and go to the right tanks, and draw samples to verify it was all done correctly. I learned how to label samples so I always did things correctly.

I also got trained on how we were to respond to any oil spills. Fortunately, we had no more than a few gallons spill into the bay during the strike, just because we got sloppy hooking up lines. But there was this one time when the dark side of the force almost succeeded in creating an event that would have been more devastating than the Exxon Valdez.

I mentioned earlier how much I admired Newton's Law of Motions in college, but I never thought I'd really see them in action. The Father of Physics surmised that force is the product of mass and acceleration (or in scientific terms: $F=ma$). Then in his third law, he said that everything pushes back with the same force it was pushed with.

I witnessed the crashing of an arriving ship, full of crude oil, into our concrete dock—even though the ship appeared to be standing still. But because of the massive mass behind it, even though the acceleration was pretty much zero, there was enough force to break through a few feet of concrete. The equal push back force put a big dent into the steel, single hull ship—but did not puncture it.

Thinking the dent could still burst open at any moment, we 'lowered the boom', and pumped off crude oil as fast as we could. A potential disaster that nobody anywhere knew about was again averted.

A BOOM, by the way, is a bunch of floats strung together that gets pulled around an oil spill to corral any oil floating on the water so it can be sopped up. Any oil that doesn't float sinks to the bottom—but that's okay since no one can see it.

Any floating oil gets sopped up using 'absorbent pads'. These industrial sized Maxi-pads are supposed to suck up oil and leave the water behind. They get thrown into the oily water, retrieved, wrung out, and thrown back in. Some of them sink to the bottom—but that's okay since no one can see them.

* * *

Since we were working so many hours, the company did bump up our pay a bit. But they mostly tried to compensate us by treating us like kings. Cigars were free for everyone (tried it, didn't like it). Can you believe it—a bunch of guys sitting in a control room, with their feet up, smoking cigars, with flammable stuff flowing all around? It happened.

And the food was the very best. The company cafeteria

turned into a gourmet restaurant. They served steak and lobster every morning and night to accommodate both shifts.

Believe it not, we all eventually got tired of eating lobster every day. But, golly, when it's free, you just have to get it. Fortunately, we found another purpose for this delicacy.

The best fishing in the entire bay was off my marine terminal. The fish seemed to like the warm 'water' we sent back into the bay. Of course, you threw back anything you caught. We all knew enough to know that you shouldn't eat anything you catch near an oil refinery. Besides, the kitchen wasn't about to let us clean and cook them anyway. But fishing was a great way to waste some of that time between shifts.

For bait, we used lobster. The fish loved it! We couldn't pull them in fast enough. We'd throw one back in, and he'd immediately turn around and bite another hook. It was crazy!

We were all having too much fun, and strike duty wasn't supposed to be fun. Management decided that the strike had to end.

* * *

Every few months, there was a Shutdown, somewhere in the refinery. For some reason, they were also called Turnarounds, although it had nothing to do with turning anything around. These were times when parts of the refinery would be shut down and everything opened up so folks could see how much damage had been done, and then make everything 'fresh' again. (That's the word they used).

There was a lot of work to do, and all of us new engineers got called in to help (more nights, weekends, and holidays). We crawled through furnaces and manholes (today I guess you'd call them people-holes, but that doesn't sound too good either)—over trays and up through columns—between pipes and through fan blades. My coveralls (they didn't really 'cover all') and I were like an industrial human toilet brush.

Yes, we cleaned everything—and replaced stuff like bubble caps and tube bundles—and looked for signs of corrosion, hot spots and the dreaded hydrogen blister. But the Turnaround was really mostly about the CATALYLST.

Instead of uranium, refinery reactors contain this dry macaroni like stuff of various brilliant colors, different shapes and sizes—some with holes, some with ridges—some of great value, some worth no more than dirt. I couldn't believe that a cup of platinum catalyst was worth more than I made in a year! (Stealing catalyst was a thing the company frowned on).

Most catalysts are very particular. They can't be packed too tight or too loose. They have to be placed carefully, not dropped. They are put into 'beds' separated by 'inert balls'. (I'm not making this stuff up!)

Some catalysts fall into their beds by sliding through long cloth tubes, with some guy at the bottom pushing around the end of the tube while wearing snowshoes that keep him from sinking into the quick sand beneath his feet. These guys are also outfitted in deep-sea diving gear because the catalyst cannot come into contact with the air. I never imagined that my first diving experience would be in nitrogen instead of water.

Other catalysts are lowered in socks into long vertical pipes. The socks are opened with a jerk, once they reach the bottom. Often, some jerk would jerk too hard and leave the sock at the bottom. It then had to be 'fished' out. Yep, hook, line and sinker. Surprising how much fight a sock can put up.

The platinum catalyst received special treatment. Since it

was so valuable, it was often refurbished instead of replaced. It got dumped, screened, roasted and reloaded. The screening fines were meticulously saved and sent off to be turned into new catalyst—that is, except the fines that ended up going down my shower drain.

When the reactors are up and running, the catalyst beds really don't do anything. They just create the ambiance for all the other stuff floating around to re-create. They provide the soft music, dim lights, and cushy 'beds' to encourage amorous activity.

What catalyst arouses is actually called REACTION KINETICS. (Still sounds sexy though, doesn't it?) And adding platinum catalyst to the scene is like giving everything the 5-Star-Hotel treatment. But since all this kinetic activity does 'soil the sheets', the beds must regularly be 'refreshed'.

* * *

After my success with the Sludge Farm, the powers-that-be thought I may be management material, and so I was given a primo job, in which I could quickly learn everything there was about the refinery. I was to help build a computer model of the refinery, and then use it to determine the best way to do things. Later, however, I learned they weren't really interested in 'the best way'. I was really expected to use the model to show that however they were doing things was 'the best way'.

The model would be an LP—not the Led Zeppelin type, but something called a Linear Program. They told me LP helped us win World War II by telling the generals where to best send troops and supplies. *Oh, so that's why we stormed the beaches of Normandy instead of somewhere else!*

I had taken one computer programming class in college. I didn't like it, and almost didn't pass. They tried to teach me something called FORTRAN IV. I guess FORTRAN I through III were failures. In my opinion, so was IV.

I remember long hours, punching cards at a keypunch machine, one statement per card. Then having to carry boxes of cards across campus after midnight to be loaded into the computer when using it was cheapest. Nope, computer programming was not for me.

For this new job, the first thing I had to do was take another computer programming class. But this time, it was very different. It was only for a week at the offices of a little computer company, where an expert in LP modeling lived. To my surprise, I took to LP modeling like a fish to lobster.

In his class, I learned that LP was really just a bunch of mathematical equations. Each equation told the model about some rule in the refinery that could not be broken. The computer then would determine how the refinery should run to not break any of these rules. Problem is, there could be thousands of ways to run the refinery without breaking any rules. The computer was to find the one very best way—the one that would make the most money, or in LP talk THE OPTIMUM. What the computer did, in LP talk, is OPTIMIZE—*which is also what General Eisenhower had done in choosing Normandy, I assumed.*

So anyway, we eventually got a model built, and it was actually making sense. Surprisingly, it was giving the answers the higher-ups were expecting. It told them they were doing everything right, just as they had hoped. I got an 'Atta Boy' and a pat on the back.

In retrospect, I realize that the refinery and LP were really just abiding by the Golden Rule: "Them who have the gold make the rules." The rules were such that the only way to run the refinery was the way they were. The real test came when I was to use the model for my own special project.

The project had to do with gasoline blending. Who knew it has to be blended? But it does. The gasoline blender follows a recipe, just like a baker—and even adds appropriate spices to the mix (dyes and detergents, not cinnamon and nutmeg).

There are different recipes for the two different gasoline 'flavors': Regular and Super. What makes them different is something called OCTANE. Super needs to have more of this than Regular.

No one really knows what octane is, only that when higher octane gasoline is used in this special engine, it 'knocks' less than when lower octane gasoline is used. Knocks are the Chugs in Chug-a-Lug-a-Lug.

So gasoline is blended by putting as much cheap, low-octane stuff into the gasoline as you can and as little expensive, high-octane stuff as you have to. The high-octane stuff is more expensive because it has received the Platinum 5-Star-Hotel treatment.

Years before, someone discovered they could fool the engines and make them knock less by adding a cheap, plentiful element to the gasoline: LEAD. This meant less of the expensive stuff had to be used. Problem was, scientists eventually realized that this lead was affecting people's brains.

"What do they want: smart kids or fast cars? They can't have both!" I heard a Higher-up actually say this in a board meeting! I also regretted having learned from my father (who had a mental breakdown in his fifties) how to (and not to) siphon gasoline by sucking on a tube.

So I was asked to use my model to determine how we were

going to stop adding lead to gasoline. The answer was obvious, use more of the 5-Star-Hotel stuff, but it would be great if my model would say something else, something cheaper.

It wouldn't, no matter what I did. The higher-ups came to an obvious conclusion: the model must be wrong, and by extension, the modeler.

I was transferred to the catalogue engineering department. After all, this is where someone with a mechanical engineering degree should be anyway.

Catalogue engineers spend their days looking up pipes, valves, and pumps in colorful vendor catalogues. They then determine how much someone else's idea to add something or pipe something differently would cost. Then they beg for the money to do it. If the higher-ups agree to pay for it, which was very seldom, they placed the orders.

It was time for me to move on.

Chapter 4
Hooked

"Like a fish to lobster"—yep, I was hooked. Big Oil likes to keep their new engineers on a steep learning curve by moving them around a lot to very different assignments—so they learn many skills, but master none. They become good at either everything, or nothing—and nobody's good at everything. I chose a different path. I wanted to become real good at one thing. I wanted to master LP modeling.

This led me to a Big Oil Corporate Office (still in California), where I would help develop an LP modeling system that several of their refineries would use. This also brought me closer to the computer than I ever thought I'd be.

I was introduced to THE MAINFRAME. This was way before the days of PCs and cell phones. I've heard it said that today's best cell phone has more computing power than yesterday's mainframes. It's probably true.

THE MAINFRAME occupied a glass room about the size of a gymnasium. Because of all the heat it generated, it had its own air conditioning system. The beast was actually made up of dozens of refrigerator sized machines with flashing lights—some sporting large reel to reel tapes. Everything was automated, so no one had to enter the cold room to change tapes or push buttons.

Folks communicated with THE MAINFRAME from TERMINALS. I'm not sure why they were called terminals, but I often felt I was at the end of something.

Most terminals were like big television tubes (not flat screens), displaying white letters on an army green background. Mom always told me not to sit too close to the TV because it could hurt my eyes. I guess sitting a foot away from these things though, was okay? Anyway, where you were typing was marked with a CURSER—appropriately named given the comments I often made.

Yes, there was a key board. I had a typing class in high school. I learned the correct fingers with which to hit each key. I had to get to forty words a minute to pass, with the keys covered so I couldn't see them if I looked. I barely made it. I now just type with two fingers and am doing just fine.

* * *

My main claim to fame in the LP world involves a technique called RECURSION. I learned what this was when I was sent away for another week of LP modeling school, given by the same expert from the Little Computer Company that I'd had years before.

Recursion basically means doing the same thing over and over again until you get it right. In our modeling system it was necessary because of something called The POOLING Problem.

So, what's the pooling problem you ask? No, it has nothing to do with billiards or swimming. Let me try to explain it by going back to gasoline blending and octane.

The low octane stuff is really not one stream, but several streams of different octane values, that get mixed (or pooled) together. The problem is, you don't know how much of each is in the mix, so you don't know the octane of the 'pool'—and so you don't know how much of the low octane pool has to be blended with the 5-Star-Hotel Stuff to make Regular or Super.

So you guess—solve the LP, find out what it said the octane of the pool ended up being, make that your next guess and solve the LP again. You keep doing this until your last guess was right. When you get there, you have CONVERGED... and can go home.

Sounds pretty easy, right? Well, the problem was: the octane of the pool often never matched what Regular and Super thought it was, so the model went insane (or as Einstein said, doing the same thing over and over again, expecting different results). You therefore never converged... or went home. That is until you were ready to give up and say, "Close enough. No one will know it's not converged anyway. The Homers must have given us bad data again."

Well, I devised a way to cure this insanity, which I called Distributed Recursion (DR). What DR does is add a few more equations (rules) to the model that keep track of something I called ERROR. The Error is the difference between the last guess and what the LP says the octane of the pool is.

So, in addition to the low octane stuff going to Regular and Super at the octane guessed, the Error is also sent (distributed) to Regular and Super. This linked the mixing of the low octane stuff directly to the portion of it going to Regular and Super for the first time, and the models converged.

DR revolutionized our LP modeling system. A couple of our refineries converted their models to use it right away, and were getting reliable, converged solutions for the first time.

Our largest refinery, though, was down on the Gulf Coast, and had never even developed an LP model. Their attitude was: "We're doin' just fine without your Yankee Bull Shit." Well, they weren't.

For reasons I still don't fully understand, other than the fact that I was still one ambitious son of a bitch, I agreed to transfer to that Gulf Coast refinery in order to build them an LP model.

* * *

What a culture shock! My wife is still trying to get over it. It wasn't just that we were moving to a small coastal town from a big city suburb, but that we were leaving a comfortable California life for the Rural South. Don't get me wrong; southern hospitality is great—until you're no longer a visitor. They saw us as city slicker Yankees coming down to tell them how things should be done.

Racism was rampant everywhere. I had never before seen real estate listings that stated 'Whites Only'. All the Blacks lived on the swampy land north of town.

Like most everyone, and because they needed the work, we had a black maid come in once a week. Mildred was fabulous. She was such a help to my wife, now a mother of three. And she was so good to the kids. We all loved her. Folks couldn't believe I asked her to watch our kids while we went away for a weekend.

The summers were hotter than we had ever known. The bugs were as big as your fist and as thick as in the biblical plagues. Termites, roaches (*HUGE* roaches), bees, hornets, crickets—we hosted all of them in our home. I had never seen anything SWARM before. Now it was an annual event.

And then there was the Pogy Plant. Some place around there made animal food out of some garbage fish. When the wind came in off the Gulf, we were treated to a rancid odor that would make your toes curl. It even drove the dogs crazy.

My daughter was born there. When I talked to my boss about

getting a few days off, I was treated to a story of how cotton pickers would stop to have their baby, then throw it on their back and keep on picking. To this day, my daughter cringes whenever I say something like, "Don't forget where you came from!"

All in all though, I kind of liked it there. I was back in my Marlon Brando 'On the Waterfront' moment. But this time, "I had class. I was a contender. I was somebody, instead of a bum."

We bought a house twice as big as we had for less than what we sold the house in California for. I was hob-knobbing with doctors and lawyers. I no longer had to commute or ride-pool. In fact, I usually went home for lunch!

And being back at a refinery again was thrilling. I hadn't realized how much I missed the action, the working folk, and even the smells.

For the most part, I eventually blended in pretty well at the refinery. I discovered I loved crawfish and oysters, which folks brought in all the time. I managed to get in with some 'Good Ol' Boys' and made some great friends.

Although most folks believed the model I was to build was not needed, it was something new. So there was a degree of excitement about it. And it received a considerable amount of attention—in the form of bets, both for and against my success.

It took about nine months to get a model built. I didn't get much help, and getting the data I needed was difficult, but the model came together and was looking pretty good. The problem was it wasn't telling folks what they wanted to hear. There was nothing anyone could say was wrong with the model, but I feared this could be Déjà vu all over again. I was right. There just had to be something wrong with the model and, by extension, the modeler. The Against folks got paid off.

This time though, they just thought I needed to learn how

things are really done around there. So they surprisingly made me the lead process engineer over a major part of the refinery. Apparently, because the best people choose not to go there, the engineering talent pool was so poor that I stood out as having potential. But I just saw it as a diversion away from what I felt I was really best at.

A few of the higher-ups had objected. "How can someone with just a mechanical engineering degree be made a process engineering lead over people with chemical engineering degrees?" The answer was to send me back to school, to take the course I dreaded at college: Organic Chemistry—night school at a local college.

* * *

My piece of the refinery had distillation, cracking, and reforming. Cracking and reforming are processes that use reactors and catalysts, which I already talked about (reforming has 5-Star-Hotel reactors), - but distillation is new.

Yep, it's basically like moonshining, where you boil fermented corn mash in a still, then cool (or distill) the vapors to get pure corn whiskey. With crude oil mash, though, you draw off different whiskeys at different cooling temperatures. The lightest whiskeys, sucked off at the lowest temperatures, are gasolines. The heavier whiskeys, sucked off at the higher temperatures, are diesel fuels. The crud left in the bottom of the still is asphalt.

However, I soon realized that being a lead process engineer was really not about the process—but about the people. I was a boss for the first time. These young, inexperienced chemical engineers working for me were actually responsible for the process. I was just to train them, guide them, and make sure everything they did was correct. Each of them had four or five projects, which meant I had twenty to thirty projects, as well as all the supervisory duties.

There was still a 'jack of all trades, master of none' mentality in refining that I found infuriating. All my engineers were expected to know everything about catalyst, furnaces, distillation, heat exchangers, compressors, utilities, etc., etc. They all knew a little about everything, but not enough about anything to do their job.

I decided to set their work responsibilities based on specific things instead of global processes. Then later, rotate them so they still get exposed to everything. Our productivity shot up, and soon other groups were doing the same thing.

But still, each engineer was different. Each had their own quirks, own work ethic, own problems, and own talents. There were four process engineering groups in the refinery – each with five or six young engineers, and one lead. So there were twenty or so young engineers.

The Big Oil Human Resource X-SPURTS (former drips under pressure) said that each year, ten percent have to go to "keep our staff strong." I lost two in the two years I was a lead—both women.

Once a year, the leads and the chief engineer met to do FORCED RANKING. This is where we each discussed the successes and failures of those working for us, then ranked them from best to worst. All the engineers were doing a good job, so one bad day that another lead happened to hear about could push someone down.

Being the newest lead, I didn't realize that I needed to also watch all the other engineers and look for faults that I could bring up at this meeting. I was also too honest about my folks compared to the other leads who tried to cover up any misdeeds. I also felt that because I had become a lead without coming up through the ranks and everyone knew I was not a chemical engineer, the other leads ganged up on me. So bottom line: both years, one of my people fell into the bottom two.

Female engineers definitely had it tougher there then. They were a minority, doing what most there still thought was a MAN'S job, and so they were constantly being watched and evaluated. One of my gals tried hard to just be 'one of the boys'—a little too hard. The Homers walked all over her, and she couldn't get them to do anything she asked. The other gal just got burned out from always being in the spotlight.

Letting them go was the hardest thing I've ever done. The tears, the pleading, the arguing, the blaming—and all I could do was try to explain the virtues of FORCED RANKING, which I completely disagreed with. Making it more difficult was the fact that I knew I too was being evaluated based on how well I handled the situation.

To add insult to injury, I did not officially fire them. They were forced to give me a letter of resignation. I had to argue that doing so would allow us to give them a favorable reference and so make it easier for them to get hired elsewhere.

In reality, doing so meant they were still legally bound to the NCA (non-compete agreement) that they did not know they had signed when they were hired. It also allowed the Big Oil company to maintain its successful recruitment rate since the company was officially not responsible for the termination. (TERMINAL: finally, the end of something I can relate to.)

Maybe, it did make it easier for them to get hired elsewhere. Hope so, since they now could not receive any unemployment benefits.

When I learned soon after the second had 'resigned' that I would be transferred, part of me was sad because I had really become good at a job I learned to like. But I was so happy to never again have to be so responsible for another colleague's livelihood.

Our Big Oil company had merged with another Big Oil company. A refinery got shut down as a result. There was a 'restructuring' plan which moved the engineers from that refinery to the others. Since I had come from somewhere else, it made sense to someone somewhere to send me back to where I came from, so one of the displaced engineers could have my job.

Chapter 5
Upstream

And then someone somewhere got a look at my history and happened to read that I was a modeler. Actually, he read LP Modeler, but not knowing what LP meant, he ignored it. It so happens that they were starting up a new group in Texas that was assigned to build a new computer modeling system for 'Upstream'. This someone thought I might be a good addition to this team.

So I was given a choice: back to California and the job I had left three years ago, or something entirely new. Since I was still an ambitious son of a bitch, I felt that going back to the job in California would be like going backwards, so I chose Texas.

I delayed telling my wife that we had to move as long as I could because I knew she disliked moving. When I finally told her we were moving to Texas, she was delighted! To her, any place was better than where we were.

A few months after we were in Texas, I casually happened to mention that we could have moved back to California. I then slept a few more nights on the couch.

So anyway, we were on our way, swimming upstream, against the crude oil current, to Texas. Until then, I hadn't realized that I had been 'downstream', or that crude oil came from 'upstream'. All I knew was that someone got this stuff, and it came to the refinery in Big Boats, from all over the world. Well, I did know from the movies that folks drilled holes in the ground to tap into big underground lakes of dead dinosaurs, and crude oil would come gushing out of the ground.

Unlike downstream, I learned that upstream, we really weren't interested in making money. Being able to sell whatever they got out of the ground was never a problem. And the Big Oil company always made sure upstream was swimming in big bucks.

But getting it out of the ground and to a place where it could be put on the Big Boats was a problem. Unexpected things always happened that caused them to not produce as much crude oil as they thought they could.

So our computer system was to show folks how they could model the upstream plumbing. How they could get their stuff out of the ground and on to the oil 'terminal' (there's that word again)—and what they had to do to avoid problems.

Well, I soon learned that lakes of dead dinosaurs do not exist. They are really rock with water, gas, and oil trapped between its particles, and that they are called reservoirs, not lakes. So the stuff gushing out of the ground is not just crude oil, but a mixture of gases, water, sand, and crude oil—and that it's gushing out of the ground at all is actually a problem our modeling system is supposed to help solve. The stuff is supposed to gush into a pipe, not into the air!

The stuff gushes because it's under pressure. How much stuff gushes and how fast depends on how much PRESSURE it's under. Get this stuff into a pipe and the 'how much' and 'how fast' becomes the RATE. So, our modeling system was supposed to somehow show the rate and pressure of the stuff anywhere in the plumbing system, reservoir to terminal. Folks could see if there were any BOTTLENECKS and do something about them.

A bottleneck is something that holds back stuff. It's good in beer bottles because you can turn one completely upside down and still chug it. Try that with a draft, and you spill beer all over your face. In upstream, you want to eliminate anything that's holding stuff back, so you can get as much stuff to the terminal as fast as possible.

The rates and pressures of the stuff change all over because of gravity, friction, and flow patterns. This last reason is the real kicker that was hard to predict.

There was no way to know how much of each thing was in the mixture at any point. But even if you did know, there was no way to know how well the things were mixed. Since the stuff was an undeterminable mixture of things -- and because gases, water, and oil all flow differently, especially when together in the same pipe -- it was impossible to say what the pressure and rate would be anywhere in the plumbing. But we did have these wonderful things called CORRELATIONS that we could use to tell us everything we'd need.

Correlations were mathematical equations that X-SPURT (which again, are former drips under pressure) scientists had developed based on testing they did. They weren't worth the paper they were written on, but we didn't know that.

There were correlations for smooth flow, correlations for turbulent flow, and correlations for slug flow. No, there weren't any slimy, blood-sucking black bugs looking for a free ride to America. Here I'm talking about 'slugs' of liquid that could pound a pipe so hard that it bursts.

I also ran into my old friend, Sir Isaac Newton, again, but this time someone had proven him wrong. Usually, when stuff is pushed, it moves as Newton decreed. But some weird things get thinner first and then move. These are called non-Newtonian fluids.

Ketchup is one. It won't move until you beat on the bottle. When you're trying to figure rates based on pressures, this stuff can drive you nuts. But you guessed it, there were correlations for it.

There were also correlations that were used for the networks—not ABC, NBC, or CBS—but the spaghetti of piping that went from the wells to the terminal.

There were more correlations for the flow of stuff through the reservoir and completion—and up the well. (The completion is cracks in the reservoir that are created by firing guns at the bottom of the well, really!)

And on top of all this, there were even correlations to tell you what correlations to use!

Early on, I was sent away to a major university to take a week-long class called Multi-phase Fluid Flow, taught by a famous professor who had developed one of the leading correlations in use. He even named the correlation after himself.

We spent a lot of time working through complicated equations that proved everything he did was correct, and why correlations developed by others weren't. We toured his lab, to see his elaborate equipment and meet all his long haired, white coated disciples.

We all left with autographed copies of his book. Most also left as excited new believers in his cause. I did not, but who am I to judge.

Pigs could also affect the calculations. No, not the 'oink oink' kind, but the kind that occasionally gets sent through pipes to clean out gunk. Sometimes gunk is good, and sometimes it's bad. But regardless, if it ain't there, things are different. Some bottlenecks disappear, and others pop up. There are no correlations for pigs.

And then there was modelling THE GOSPs. These are big vessels (remember? big cylindrical things?) that separate most of the gas from the oil at crucial points in the networks.

The gas is worthless, so you need to get rid of it. So, what can you do with it? Well, sometimes it's flared (remember those?) But more often, it's just vented. After all, "it ain't nothin' but the same stuff a cow farts. So it's natural and won't hurt anything."

Well, over the next two years, we managed to put together a modeling system. It ran and spit out numbers. It was impossible to say it was right, but it was also impossible to say it was wrong, so they used it, all around the world. The upstream world was just so thankful to have something that would give them some guidance. It didn't really matter if it was correct. No one would know.

They were especially pleased with it in Saudi Arabia, since it told them they had no bottlenecks.

* * *

A couple of the others on my team, as well as my bosses, were bona fide petroleum engineers, some even doctors of the profession. These were super chemical engineers who specialized in Upstream. They knew a lot but didn't seem to work very hard.

The computer program itself was very complicated and could not be deciphered by any normal human being. It had been written by X-SPURT programmers using the latest computer techniques, under the close direction of X-SPURT (evil?) scientists. Yes, it was a monster.

The difficult thing now, though, was teaching the lesser

engineers, called production engineers, how to use it. They were the ones who actually had to do something about the bottlenecks it might find. Being a lesser engineer myself, it was felt I could communicate better with them. So, I was assigned to write the user manuals and conduct the training courses.

I, therefore, became the face of the program -- and the bosses didn't like that. But since my training courses were receiving rave reviews, and the modelling program was becoming a hit in the field, they couldn't do anything about it.

For all my efforts, I really should have been promoted. Thanks to me, my boss was. He became the upstream vice president of South America. I should have at least been moved into his job. But this would have placed me, a mechanical engineer with just a four-year degree from a no-name college, above folks with doctorates in petroleum engineering from schools like Texas A&M. That could not happen. I was stuck.

But I would be temporarily made the acting leader of the group without being promoted until they found someone more 'qualified'. There was no one else who knew enough about everything to manage the group.

I knew the assignment would be short. I also knew they had no idea what to do with me after that.

* * *

They really liked me in Saudi Arabia. The bosses saw that as a way to solve their problem with me. So I was 'offered' the 'opportunity' to move to Saudi Arabia.

I had been there several times to conduct training classes. Didn't like it. They were still chopping off hands for stealing! One time, people were still talking about the public hanging the week before.

If your cab driver got into a wreck, it was your fault. Thinking was, if you weren't there, it wouldn't have happened! Most of the cabbies were driving camels only a few weeks before, so this was a major cause of concern.

I had a cab driver once who insisted on looking at me in the back seat - head turned, one hand on the wheel and the other over the seat—while he talked and talked and drove. I knew if I said anything, he'd stop and put me out. So I just sat there and silently prayed, which was also forbidden.

We passed guys draped in white, followed by their many wives draped in black—and we passed gold shops galore. Saudi guys bought their wives lots of gold bangles and things. These were their only retirement plan, or more often, divorce alimony.

I brought my wife back an 18-karat gold puzzle ring once. These are actually five rings in one, elaborately entwined. The Saudis used them for wedding rings. If the bride took it off, the rings fell apart, and there was no way a WOMAN could put them back together, so the husband would know she removed them. My wife had hers welded together.

There were more freedoms on the compound where all the Expats lived (foreigners the Saudis brought in to run things—I too could now become one!). They tried to make the compound like a Little America. But hearing the 'calls to prayer' belted out several times a day from loud speakers positioned in the sky reminded you that you ain't in Kansas anymore.

Bacon was not allowed anywhere. I was never a big fan of bacon, but when you can't have it, you crave it. Like most everything else Americans eat, the creative compound cafeteria chefs managed to come up with something that looked like bacon, but it sure wasn't bacon.

Alcohol was forbidden. They'd even confiscate mouthwash at the airport (along with Bibles and crosses, and passports if you'd ever been to Israel). But all the expats had a still in their garage, and the authorities would look the other way (for a pint or two). The chemical engineers there really knew how to make good stuff!

As students in my class, the expats were very good. Most of the students in the class, however, were Saudis, and they didn't know what they were doing. But they were really just there for me to sign their attendance sheet. Once I did, they were gone. Most had the word 'Prince' before their names.

The Saudis also insisted I give them a course completion certificate signed by me to hang on their wall. So far, no one has come after me for their not having learned anything.

There's actually not a lot for the engineers there to do since the answer to every problem is to spend as much as you want. So, they spent most of their time in their cushy high-rise offices, planning their next vacation. They were getting boo coos of extra, tax-free cash, six weeks of guaranteed vacation leave, and cheap flights to Europe or Southeast Asia. Who wouldn't want that? Me.

So anyway, I had the 'opportunity' to join this paradise. As a new expat, I'd be assigned to live in one of the glorious trailers at the edge of the compound, with the entire desert as my backyard. My son would get to enroll in a boarding school in Europe or the US since there were no high schools in the compound.

I tried to make them promise that the Saudi assignment would be no more than three years, and that I was guaranteed a promotion upon my return. They would agree to neither. Seeing no choice, I took the job—then immediately started looking for another.

Since I was still the acting lead of the group, my exit interview was conducted by the guy who had been my boss's boss. This was the same guy who originally put our group together and brought me in five years before. He had lured me into his vision of modelling upstream, promising me professional recognition and advancement opportunities. Thanks substantially to my efforts, his vision was achieved, but I was to be exiled.

He was pissed that I didn't want to go to Saudi Arabia. I was pissed that I was being screwed. I told him the company's claim that "its most important asset is its employees" was BULL SHIT. He said I was indecisive, to which I replied, "I'm indecisive? I'M INDECISIVE? I QUIT, DIDN'T I?"

Well, at least I had become fully vested in the company's retirement plan only a week before.

Chapter 6
Back Downstream

"Ohooooo-kla-hom-ma, where the wind comes sweepin' down the plain." Yeeow! I finally got back downstream—back to LP modeling—this time in the corporate office of a Mid-sized Oil company in Sooner Land.

I did call around to some friends in downstream at my last company before I quit, to see if there was any way I could get back. There wasn't. I had been out of their people mill too long. Since I was promoted when I became a lead engineer, my rank was too high for any positions they might have open. And there were plenty of candidates for any jobs at my rank that hadn't been away for five years.

The wife still agreed to follow this ambitious son of a bitch. She was also for getting out of the Texas heat, and back to a place with four seasons. The kids were all happy, and doing better in school, since they were easier than (and not as good as) schools in Texas. Me? I was back in my groove and feeling fine.

Working in the corporate office of a smaller oil company got me a lot closer to the action, and the Big Wigs. I was regularly attending meetings with VPs and the CEO in the board room, to discuss company strategies that were suggested by my model. I was also regularly talking with the Crude Oil Traders, who were making multi-million-dollar deals based on what my model told them.

Little had changed while I was away. Everyone did have

desktop computers now instead of mainframe terminals, but they didn't seem to work any better. LP modeling was pretty much the same, if not worse. My new company hadn't yet started using Distributed Recursion. Could that be one reason they scooped me up?

Nope, they'd never heard of it. It turned out that my old company considered it 'proprietary' (secret) and didn't want anyone else to know about. They liked that others were still not using recursion, or if they were, they were struggling with convergence. Their thinking was that DR gave them a competitive advantage because, without it, other companies would make poorer decisions.

As luck would have it, my new company was using an LP modeling system that was being maintained by the same little computer company that had taught me LP modeling all those years before. They had made some progress in recursion but were meeting resistance because the models would not converge. Most everyone, including us, were still modeling without pooling, letting everything go to everywhere, even though there weren't pipes in the real refinery to actually do that.

* * *

I learned that the industry had finally removed Lead from gasoline. But in a quest to still avoid giving more gasoline the 5-Star-Hotel treatment, some X-SPURT scientist discovered that Lead could be replaced by another element: Manganese.

Unfortunately, Manganese also had problems. Instead of making people dumb like lead had, it gave some people 'the shakes'. After a few years, folks agreed that that probably wasn't a good thing either, so they decided to stop using Manganese in gasoline too.

So now what? Well, the story goes that somewhere in Texas, another scientist (who moonlighted as a bar-tender nights and weekends) put some booze together with some other horrid stuff and created a magic Elixir he called MTB. (He was listening to *'Fire on the Mountain'* by the Marshall Tucker Band at the time.) Unfortunately though, it tasted like shit. Not wanting to waste it, he poured it into his gas tank and drove home. His clunker purred like a kitten for the first time, all the way home.

MTB Elixir wasn't quite as good as lead at reducing the 'knocks', but using it did mean that less of the 5-Star-Hotel stuff had to be used. MTB Elixir didn't cause 'the shakes', or make people dumb, unless you threw back a shot of it and chased it with a beer. MTB Elixir definitely required a beer chaser since it tasted like shit by itself. Believe it or not, that was also its problem when it was blended with gasoline.

Who would ever drink MTB Elixir mixed in gasoline, you ask? Good question. But that was exactly what was happening. The stuff was leaking out of underground tanks at gas stations all over the country, and getting into the groundwater.

I was surprised to hear that anything was leaking from those buried tanks! Anyway, it only took a smidgen of this stuff to make the water for miles around taste bad. The water was still safe to drink (so we were told)—just yucky.

"What's wrong with water tasting a little funny?"—a comment I actually overheard in the board room. Well, the evil bureaucrats in government's Environmental Protection Agency (EPA) saw a lot wrong with it, and so they banned MTB Elixir from gasoline.

But they did like the idea of putting booze in cars (gas tanks, not drivers). They liked that it was RENEWABLE, which basically meant it didn't come from crude oil. So, was there a good tasting booze that could be used instead? You bet! MOONSHINE—real corn whiskey.

Farmers loved the idea. Making corn whisky for gasoline took a lot of corn, so its price would go up and they'd make a lot more money. Of course, the Jolly Green Giant would also have to raise his corn price, which wouldn't make shoppers happy, but they could eat beans instead.

Oil companies weren't as crazy about the idea. They pointed out that moonshine wasn't as good as gasoline, so folks wouldn't get as many miles per gallon. They also pointed out that if you tried to put too much moonshine into gasoline, cars would explode. But they liked that mixing in some moonshine would mean they wouldn't have to use as much of the 5-Star-Hotel stuff, so they agreed to give it a go.

I liked the idea. Here I was helping to clean up the world by replacing fossil fuels with a renewable. Using my LP model, we determined that about a gallon of moonshine could be mixed in ten gallons of gasoline before a car would explode.

* * *

The company had only one gigantic refinery on the Gulf Coast, not far from where I had worked before. I spent a lot of time going down there to meet with folks that agreed and disagreed with my model.

Often, I got to go down on the company jet with the Big Wigs! The plane was fully stocked and even included nice ladies passing out drinks. They'd usually drop me off at the refinery, then fly on to Florida.

At the time, companies like mine were having a hard time

getting crude oil. My new company didn't have its own 'upstream' crude oil like the other companies I had worked for. They had to buy theirs.

Someone had worked out a sweetheart deal with some corrupt country with a lot of crappy crude oil. Instead of paying this country what the world was saying their crude oil was worth, we would pay them whatever my model said it's worth plus a fixed profit. The deal made the corrupt country politicians much more money than they would have gotten otherwise, as well as saved our company from bankruptcy.

Crude oil comes in many different colors, thicknesses, and 'flavors'. It can be anywhere from as clear as water to as black as coal—and every shade of brown in between—with some greens, blues, and grays occasionally mixed in here and there for effect. Crude oil can be as thin as water or as stiff as putty. and smell as sweet as a rose or as bad as a rotten egg.

Unlike a fine wine, crude oil being 'sweet' or 'dry' is not depending on the amount of sugar in it, but on the amount of sulfur. Instead of 'dry' though, un-sweet crude oil is called 'sour'. Only crappy wines are called 'sour', sweet or dry.

I can't remember ever actually tasting the stuff, but the sour crude oil sure did stink a lot more. Our sweetheart deal was for the nastiest, thickest, sourest, darkest substance that ever came forth from the depths of the Earth.

After a year or so, things changed, as they often do when dealing with oil cartels. We could now easily buy other crude oils again. So I was asked to use my model each month to create what was called a 'hit list' of available crude oils. This list ranked crude oils based on how much money we could make running them.

I found many crude oils that would make us more money

than the sweetheart deal, and I did so, repeatedly. When I told the crude traders about them, they bought them, and made us a lot of money.

Needless to say, this pissed off the people who had made the sweetheart deal, as well as the corrupt country politicians who had a guaranteed fixed profit for selling us their crap. As a result, I was now on their 'hit list'.

Sure, I was only doing my job, but somehow, I was the ambitious son of the bitch who went out on his own and screwed up the deal. Never mind the success. This was political.

About the same time, my new boss learned I was making more money than he was. That's never a good thing. He too, wanted me gone.

Funny that my old boss, who had instructed me to do better than the sweetheart deal if I could, was no longer there. He had been promoted to manager of the refinery, based on all the success his group brought to the company. I believe he threw me under the bus on his way out.

To save my life, there was talk about me also going to the refinery. I could be hidden in its bowels until it was safe to come back. If they were sending me to Sicily like they did Michael Corleone, I might have considered it.

But there was no way my family would take the culture shock of another move to the Gulf Coast. In fact, getting them to leave Oklahoma would be difficult. We had a nice home, great friends, and happy kids involved in all sorts of things. The weather was great, and my wife loved her job teaching pre-school. She still says it was her favorite place of everywhere we've lived.

But I had to get the hell out of Dodge.

Chapter 7
My Sweet Spot

Well, it took a while, but I finally learned to read the writing on the wall (maybe that DNA thing had still been dumbing my absorption of knowledge). I knew a move was in my future when I suddenly got a new boss. So I decided then to go for the job I'd always wanted—joining the LP modeling expert who taught me the craft all those years ago in the Little Computer Company he had helped start thirty years before.

Each year, the Little Computer Company held what they called a User's Meeting. It attracted people from all over the world, who were using their LP modeling software.

I hadn't been to one of these meetings in years. Although they used the Little Computer Company's software, my current company had never sent anyone before because of the cost. My new boss didn't know that. He okayed it, and I was off... to interview.

A week later, I was working for the Little Computer Company, had the house on the market—and, although we would be moving back to Texas, I was on a plane to Taiwan. When I tried to give the standard thirty-day notice, the new boss said. "You're no good to me now. Get the hell out of here."

He was such a creep. I ran into him again, years later. He was all smiles and said how good it was to see me. He was now working in a lesser job for another, even smaller company.

* * *

The family eventually succumbed to follow their ambitious son of a bitch one last time. They did not realize that, in fact, my ambition had softened a bit. I had gotten to where I wanted. I had found my sweet spot in the oil industry cesspool.

The Little Computer Company's structure was such that nobody really worked for anyone else. Even the Little Computer Company's president was doing what everyone else was, and didn't really care what everyone else was doing. He was 'Dad', and everyone respected him immensely, but he let all us kids go our merry way. Yes, the Little Computer Company was itself a private, family-owned firm, and it was run like a family.

So there was really no 'moving up' in the company, and no reason for me to continue being a son of a bitch (well, I still was anyway). Each person took on their own responsibility. Since everyone there had already been through all the bull shit, and were then carefully invited to become a family member, there was no question that they could make it on their own. It all worked marvelously.

The job required a lot of travel, both domestic and international. In the earlier years, I was gone at least one week every month, usually for two-week periods.

I've been to fifty-six countries and forty-eight states. I've gone around the world twice, just because that was the cheapest way to go. I've flown over the North Pole, around a refinery on fire, and through a desert sand storm.

I've been greeted by scantily clad women offering leis and camouflaged soldiers holding AK47s. I've been detained, propositioned, and hospitalized. I've jumped onto a moving boat, been pulled in a rickshaw, and bounced on a camel's back.

I've been to the deserts of Arabia, the tar sands of Alberta, and oil platforms off California's coast. I've walked on glaciers in the Canadian Rockies, through volcano ash fields in the Philippines, and over the Great Wall of China. I've seen the fjords in Norway, the Eiffel Tower in Paris, the Parthenon in Athens, the pyramids in Egypt and the Wailing Wall in Jerusalem. I could go on and on and on, but this isn't supposed to be a travel book.

The trips were to help people with their models, teach people how to model, build new models, ask people to try modeling, or attend conferences where I'd often give a presentation. It was good to be working with Big Oil companies now, instead of for them, but the travel was grueling.

I was surprised at the number of companies that didn't think they needed a model. They didn't feel they needed to have some computer tell them what is best to do. Their country, or boss, or gut always told them what to do and they did it!

Some companies thought that since they always did everything the same way or always fed the same crude oils, what's there to improve? Others said that it didn't really matter if they made or lost money, since the government just expected them to provide jobs. These companies tended to have thousands of employees, some whose only job was to open or close a single valve when told.

So I spent a lot of time just teaching the refinery staff and their bosses why they should want to make more money. Why changing the way they did things to take advantage of world markets and prices would help them succeed. How proper planning would allow them to take shutdowns without passing on major disruptions to themselves or their customers.

In retrospect, I don't know if all my lessons on Western

capitalism were such a good thing. Everyone was so happy before. Now everyone was stressed out because bosses were on their butts, pushing them for that last cent of profit. Competition was now something they had to beat instead of cooperate with. They also realized they could do better with fewer employees and more automation.

* * *

The other side of my job was to improve our computer programs. My first task was to get Distributed Recursion (DR) working in the company's modeling system. To do so, I had to first get people to accept pooling and the idea of recursion—and to believe that doing things over and over again *can* give different results.

Notice I said *different*, not better. That was part of the problem. The old dumb models thought everything could go anywhere, and so always sent the best stuff to the best places. They, therefore, always said they could make more money than they really could. Recursion models with DR told them what they could actually do, and how much money they could actually make, which was never as much.

The guys I was working with were the dreamers of oil refining, the PLANNERS. They were planning what to do thirty or so days from now based on strategies sent from above. They worked hard to give their superiors a rosy picture of the future so they would be happy and treat them nice.

They had nothing to do with what happened when the time they planned for actually came. It was then up to the SCHEDULERS to make their dreams come true.

Schedulers were Homers who just wanted to keep things

going. They never did as well as the planners had predicted. They blamed the planners, and the planners blamed them.

The planners were always able to explain that the differences had nothing to do with them by pointing to other reasons. There were always problems around at the time when things actually had to get done. Equipment broke down. Ships were late. Stuff got mixed wrong. The weather was bad. You name it.

All these were fine and good reasons for the schedulers to not meet the plan. But planners thinking their models were telling them the truth when they weren't was the main reason. The schedulers continued to believe this, no matter what the planners said.

Most planners I met saw no reason to change their models and get less profitable results. It wouldn't look as good to their bosses, who use the numbers to show their governments, or stockholders, or buddies how well they were doing. It took a good five years, and usually a new generation of planners before a few of them were using DR.

Then I got some unexpected help. The dreaded EPA added a new novel regulation that could only be modeled with recursion. This brought the others over.

* * *

When I was with the Big Oil companies, I was taught that the EPA was my arch enemy. Now, they were sort of an ally. In fact, they were using our system to model the effects of their regulations so they would know if the Big Oil companies were telling them the truth.

The EPA came up with something they called REFORMULATED gasoline. Reformulated gasoline required gasoline to be defined by something called TOXICITY. (So, gasoline without lead is still toxic? My siphoning mishaps returned to haunt me).

Unlike octane, you could not determine gasoline toxicity based on what was blended into it. The amount of low-octane stuff, or 5-Star-Hotel stuff, didn't matter; it was all toxic. The toxicity did not depend on what went into the Regular and Super, but on a car's exhaust from burning it.

The EPA did though, give us several complicated equations so we could calculate toxicity. The equations were basically some more correlations that meant something to somebody somewhere. But since they had been developed by the government, these correlations must be correct.

So here I was with another chance to help 'clean up the world'. I would model toxicity. Refineries would still make Regular and Super of X toxicity, no more and no less. But this time, the EPA would reduce X each year, forcing things to get cleaner.

To model toxicity, I came up with a new kind of recursion that I called Adherent Recursion (AR). I called it Adherent because it mathematically stuck to the EPA's screwy equations. AR piggy-backed on DR. This meant that toxicity could only be modeled in recursion models.

So, to model toxicity using AR, clients had to change their models to use DR. Once they did, both DR and AR took off.

They began to use it for all sorts of things in their models. They were able to now OPTIMIZE those astronomical reactor temperatures and pressures – and the distillation temperatures for gasoline, diesel, and asphalt—and so many other things. Just as that other kind of LP gave way to music you could download, my kind of LP has become a kind of artificial intelligence. And surprise, surprise, the schedulers were able to come closer to what the planners had predicted.

But differences still remained. And the schedulers could no longer blame them on the planners. These differences were really due to the time things actually had to get done and all the other crap that goes on in a bustling oil refinery.

* * *

Planners plan things based on the HOW MUCHes. How much crude oil are we going to get this month? How much Super and Regular are we going to make this month? Schedulers are more concerned with the WHENs. When does the crude oil ship come in? When do we have to send the Regular or Super to the stations? The WHENs can't be done if the HOW MUCHes aren't done yet.

I like to say that planning is like a map. It shows you the route to go from where you are to where you're going, and the miles in between. You can then estimate the time it will take.

Scheduling is like a GPS. It knows where you want to go but only shows you where you are and doesn't really know that you can get to where you want at the time you want. It can't tell you what the weather is going to be like along the route or if there might be an accident that slows you down.

Schedulers have to know how to 'reroute' around accidents, or construction, or things being late, and do so to arrive as close to the time that the planners predicted as possible. Poor scheduling can destroy the best laid of plans—and all that great LP modeling work that I had devoted my career to.

So this scheduling problem was to be my next nut to crack. My New Frontier. LP modeling was now in pretty good shape. Folks were still coming up with more things that could be done with DR and AR and how to do it all faster, but my work there was pretty much done. So I made scheduling my new challenge.

But what could I do? LP modeling determines the best way to do things to make the most money. But at the time of scheduling, the money decisions have already been made. Making money has nothing to do with anything. The Homers just want to know what they must do to make it all work.

Well, we came up with a great computer program that showed the Homers with colorful charts and graphs where, in GPS terms, they were at. Then it let them look into the future and see if they could deal with stuff that was supposed to happen. Then it showed them the consequences of anything they might try to 'reroute' the operation.

But they still had to work as hard. They still had to decide themselves what to do and when to do it. And now there were pretty pictures to show them, their bosses, and everyone else the mistakes they made, in Technicolor, no less.

Homers… would rather just be Homers—sit back, put their feet up, and puff on their cigars. If scheduling was to be modeled, we'd have to model the Homers.

But how? Well, the Homers did have these things called 'Rules of Thumb'. When they used their thumb rules correctly, they actually did a pretty good job. Problem was, they had trouble following their own rules.

They learned their Thumb Rules over many years of Trial and Error (mostly error). This is where they'd say, 'Let's try this!' If it worked, thumbs up—if it didn't, thumbs down.

Problem was, they had so many thumb rules that they didn't know which ones to use when. Some thumb rules were only thumbs up if other thumb rules were also thumbs up; otherwise, they might be thumbs down. The whole situation was very complicated.

Okay, so "let's put the thumb rules into the computer program and let the computer decide which ones to follow when." Well, we did that, and it worked very well. But then we had problems getting the Homers to believe the computer was telling them what they would actually do.

We also discovered that each refinery had come up with its own 'Rules of Thumb', and they weren't the same for everybody everywhere every time. Well, we went ahead and added all these other thumb rules to the computer program, as well as any others anyone might dream up. Now the computer program was also very complicated.

That's pretty much as far as I got with scheduling. Some schedulers are using the computer program and really like it. Others, though, just want to say they're so good that they can beat the computer. They claim they can always come up with a better solution on their own – and often, they can.

Well, the program isn't for everybody everywhere every time, yet. The work continues, but the time had come for me to 'hang up my gear'.

Chapter 8
Home

"County roads, take me home." So after fifty years of grunts and grinds, rants and rage, trials and tribulations, I was on my way to a well-earned retirement. My wife and I did not want to spend our golden years in hot, flat Texas, so we moved to West Virginia.

It's a beautiful state and a great place to retire. My folks met here at a family reunion. Might explain that DNA thing.

Unlike most of the newly liberated, I had hoped my retirement would not include 'seeing the world'. I am so glad to be rid of the airport hassles, the rental car complications, the shysters at every turn, and the hotel life. But since there's still a few places my wife would like to see, and she's now making all the decisions on where we go, I imagine the 'Friendly Skies' may still be in my future.

After retiring, though, I did want to try some new things, meet some new people, maybe do some real fishing, get more involved in community affairs, and spend more time with my family and friends. But two months after receiving my last pay check, I was at home, locked in like everyone else, because some Homer somewhere didn't close the door and let the COVID out.

I still managed to take up some new things. I now play an instrument, am a chess master (the last creative embellishment in this book). I got an RV for camping and learned how to fiddle with some of those bucks I didn't know I had before I retired. I am now also (not by choice) an X-SPURT on Medicare coverage. And I have discovered that my true calling may have actually been in hospitality.

I was never a super student, super engineer, or super father, but I am now a super host. I have finally fully embraced management... of my own Air BNB condominium. I am finding that this endeavor is requiring many of the skills I have acquired over my career and is paying me considerably more than I made in my first job after college.

But even with all these admirable senior citizen occupations, I have found myself still restless, still interested in what was happening in refining, and still wishing to help 'clean up the world'.

I recently learned that the first place I worked, the place with Forrest and my sludge farm, was going green. They were going out of the crude oil business entirely and were instead planning to turn vegetable oils into diesel fuel. It got me thinking.

Why were they doing this? Was it because they weren't allowed to farm sludge anymore? I doubted that. Hopefully, someone made them stop doing that years ago.

So I dug around and found an article about it. The article said they were doing it to reduce the Greenhouse Gases (GHG) that are causing climate change.

Greenhouse Gases are gases that trap heat. They get the name from greenhouses because that's what greenhouses do (not because greenhouses are full of bad gas). A greenhouse is all windows that let in sunlight. The sunlight creates warmth, and the greenhouse keeps it from leaving.

Greenhouse gases in the air do the same thing. They let sunlight pass in and heat things up, but then they prevent the heat from leaving. Really, greenhouse gases are a good thing. Without them, the world would be too cold, and life as we know it would not exist. But there's now too much of a good thing. Especially too much of the two worse GHGs: carbon dioxide and methane.

What could be wrong with carbon dioxide, you ask? It's true that plants live on the stuff. But again, it's a 'too much of a good thing' thing. Back in the 1800s, only 0.028 percent of the air was carbon dioxide. Now it's 0.042 percent, nearly twice as much. Still doesn't seem like much, though, does it? Unless you're a glacier.

Methane 'ain't nothin' but cow farts'. Remember that? It's also the stuff that kills canaries in coal mines. As a GHG, it's eighty times worse than carbon dioxide.

The EPA will soon set something called Carbon Intensity rules on refineries. This is sort of a 'cow farts per gallon of crude oil' number. It will account for all the carbon dioxide and methane released at GOSPs and flares, as well as trucks, boats, and everything else that has anything to do with getting the crude oil from the reservoir to the refinery. This number may well make LP models one day say refineries will lose money if they process crude oil.

The place I used to work has the right idea: to make diesel fuel from vegetable oils. But there just ain't enough of that stuff around, and it's already being used for other things. I wondered if there was any way we could get more oil out of vegetables— oil that might not be good enough for the other things (like food and feed), but good enough for refineries to turn into diesel fuels. There is!

Vegetable oils are squeezed out of things like corn, peanuts, sunflower seeds, and soy beans. But there is still so much energy left in the rest of these plants after the best parts are gone – in the husks, the cobs, the stalks, the leaves. This energy is not like what's in the cooking oils from the best parts of the plants, but like what's in the stuff made by dissolving the rest of the plant.

Turns out that all these other parts of the plant have some sugar in them. Saps and nectars are in every plant in some form. And just like a kid who has pigged out on pancakes, or a humming bird beating its wings, this sugar is energy.

This energy is now being wasted. It is the energy released when those parts of the plant degrade – the kind of energy that makes a compost pile get hot. Remember the 2nd Law of Thermodynamics from my college days: energy can be changed, but not made? Why not change compost energy into stuff that powers engines?

When these plant parts are dissolved in acid, the sugar is busted into weird pieces of organic materials. Then, in beds of catalyst, where the perfect ambience has been created, these pieces gloriously come together differently to conceive... Baby Diesel. (Brings a tear to your eye, doesn't it?)

* * *

So this is what I'm working on now—not for pay, just for fun. It's so liberating to be doing something not because someone's paying me to, or because a client demands it, or because someone else's livelihood depends on it, but just because I can do something that just might help make the world a cleaner place.

squeek!

Printed in the USA
CPSIA information can be obtained
at www.ICGtesting.com
CBHW020206301124
18173CB00042B/448